T0131505

# I AM Worthy

## I AM HEALED

### Kathryn Bonney

**BALBOA.**
PRESS

A DIVISION OF HAY HOUSE

Scripture taken from the King James Version of the Bible.

Balboa Press books may be ordered through booksellers or by contacting:

Balboa Press
A Division of Hay House
1663 Liberty Drive
Bloomington, IN 47403
www.balboapress.com
1 (877) 407-4847

Print information available on the last page.

ISBN: 978-1-5043-4826-3 (sc)
ISBN: 978-1-5043-4841-6 (hc)
ISBN: 978-1-5043-4827-0 (e)

Library of Congress Control Number: 2016900580

Balboa Press rev. date:  06/21/2016

# Contents

I dedicate this book to my family: Charles (my husband); William, Richard, and Kristine (our children); Brian Moran (our son-in-law); Jack and Matthew (our grandsons); and Megan, Kaitlin, and Brooke (our granddaughters).

# Foreword

Kathy and I met many years ago selling collectibles at an antique shop. Over time she began to experience some breathing problems that turned out to be COPD, so she had to move on. We stayed in touch, but as time passed, the phone calls and the visits got shorter.

Kathy believes in the power of self-healing, and in a small amount of time she accomplished a lot. She found tools that served her mission, believed in herself, never quit, and held on to her strong spiritual beliefs.

When you get into this wonderful book, you will feel her spirit of hope and trust in a higher way. Her message is clear: no matter how bad things are, we can improve them if we don't give up and believe anything is possible.

J. Hallberg

Author of *Invoking the Spirit*

# Acknowledgments

Thanks, Chuck, for your help and understanding during my writing months and also for enjoying all of the hot dog and beans dinners. A special thanks to my friends—Mary Lou Dabbs, for typing the manuscript, and author J. Hallberg, for writing the foreword.

# Introduction

To my readers:

I have written this book for those looking for answers to complete the puzzle of life. Many will gain knowledge of how a positive attitude toward yourself and others relates to Bible scriptures.

You will be reading about my beliefs and also my results from meditation. I suggest my book should be studied and read repeatedly after the first reading. I predict positive changes in your life when the directions in this book are followed.

I am projecting success and love,
Kathryn Bonney

# *Part 1*

My African violets and the two of us moved to Elgin from Des Plaines in 1998. Our children were happily married, and we waited for grandchildren as Chuck golfed and I shopped.

I was checking an antique store near Elgin called the Upstairs/ Downstairs Shoppe when I met Jennie Hallberg, who was an antique dealer. Only a few days later I decided to be a dealer too! Antiques are also my hobby.

Jennie and I not only worked together but talked about poetry, writing, and spiritual growth. Our friendship grew in the next few years until I closed my business after I was diagnosed with emphysema, also known as COPD.

Jennie and I became close friends again three years later. We shared spiritual growth, and I discussed all of my experiences with her, sharing the way issues I had always developed into spiritual growth in the future. She said, "Kathy, put it on paper. Write a book." Months passed until I decided she was right. If others can benefit from my experiences then yes, I will tell my story.

# My Childhood

I experienced many things in childhood. They happened for a reason, and I believe without them, I may not have had the opportunity to begin my spiritual journey, which started thirty three years later.

My mom gave birth to me in our home, which was equipped with a coal stove and outdoor plumbing. The year was 1938, and we lived in a small town in southern Indiana.

In my toddler years I played with my brother, Charles, until Dad decided Charles needed to be disciplined. Dad used either a yardstick or willow switch to torture him. I remember crying with my brother as he was trying to hold back his tears.

Dad was always angry, and he had a couple of sayings: "This is going to hurt me more than it does you" or "Spare the rod and spoil the child."

My first whipping was given by Grandpa. I was staying with my grandparents overnight, and I had been crying for my mother.

Grandpa threatened to whip me if I didn't shut up. I didn't believe him. He reached for the yardstick, and I got my first "licking." I was only three and a half years old. We were never good friends after that.

Dad told Mom many times, "Never tell them they're good. Never give them compliments. They will only get a big head."

A teenage boy molested me when I was seven. The teenager's parents were members of our church. Mom would have been embarrassed and Dad would have blamed me, so I decided to forget the incident. I was in my thirties when I remembered.

The whippings continued, even longer, and I wasn't allowed to cry. If I did, Dad threatened to hit harder.

I had nightmares most nights. One dream I repeatedly had was being in the center of a whirlpool of water watching the water and thinking I was drowning. Even though I took swimming lessons in my twenties, I hesitated to be near water. Did I drown in another life?

Asking why was a daily question. I only heard laughs or "Be quiet." Dad thought he was being polite by not saying, "Shut up."

My walks from church every Sunday were not pleasant. My head was full of fear, not wanting to see hell. I thought, *I must be bad. Dad thinks I am.*

Bedroom doors were always open. I could not be by myself. If I closed the door, Mom opened it, and I'd be scolded.

One day I knelt by the side of my bed to ask God why I felt so horrible and asked him to guide me. Mom was embarrassed as she saw me kneeling, knowing she had disrupted my prayers.

I was called an overgrown cow, unworthy, not serving, and dumb. I was told I would never be liked and that I was fat as a pig. My dad was a butcher. He killed pigs and cows, and I felt he grouped me with them. I never missed love because I never experienced it. I thought all homes were like mine, and I just couldn't be good enough for my parents.

I was never allowed to cry, not even at funerals. My grandpa died when I was fourteen years old. I was showing emotion at his funeral until my mom insisted I stop crying. I thought it was a great time to shed tears for a pet that had recently died.

I still wanted to get my dad's approval. I saw how other dads treated their daughters, so I tried harder, trying to talk to him, rubbing his neck or combing his hair. He seemed like he enjoyed the neck rub but never acknowledged my attempt to get a thank you.

When I was in my teens, my hurt turned to resentment, and I tried to ignore my father whenever possible.

In high school my life was better. I'd outgrown whippings, but my dreams of having a boyfriend or being a cheerleader didn't come true. Dad's dream came true, though. He insisted I play the clarinet in the high school band. Once again he destroyed the chances of me taking lessons on the drums. We were all victims.

Charles graduated from high school, and in the fall he entered Indiana University.

Mom's thoughts on women attending college were as follows:

- Women need not waste time or money on college because they are going to be married. Their husbands can care for them.
- After marriage women should stay home and care for the family.
- If a woman wants to go to a trade school, that's okay.

A few words of wisdom my mother offered:

- Be happy for others.
- Always look at the bright side of life.
- Give and you will receive.
- You can become anything you want.
- Always be happy.

After my high school graduation in 1956, I decided to move to Chicago and learn hairstyling. Mom was happy. She had encouraged me to learn a trade and move away. Dad was not happy. He complained about money and said everyone in Chicago was probably a gangster. Finally he saw I was determined to leave. His attitude changed.

He said, "Okay leave, but you'll be back in three months." At that moment I realized he wanted me to fail!

Childish thoughts of "I'll show you" were in my mind as the bus took me to my new home. I made friends easily, and they helped me advance in the world of hairstyling. I entered two hairstyling competitions and won first place in both. I became successful in my career.

> Why early childhood has such a significant impact on our emotional, mental and physical well-being through our adult years.

> The fundamental behaviors, beliefs, and attitudes become "hard-wired" as synaptic pathways in our subconscious minds. Once programmed into the subconscious mind, they control our biology for the rest of our lives ... unless we can figure out a way to reprogram them.

> Bruce Lipton, *The Biology of Belief* (Carlsbad, CA: Hay House, Inc.)

> Nick Ornter, The Tapping Solution (Carlsbad, Ca.: Hay House, Inc.)

> The adverse childhood experiences (ace Study) a research project funded by Kaiser Permanente and the Centers for Disease Control confirms the lasting impact on early childhood.

The study also confirmed direct correlations between childhood trauma and cancer, heart disease, stroke, high blood pressure, bone fracture, depression and drug use. Many of the study participants were over 60 years of age.

I met Charles Bonney, my soon-to-be husband, in 1960. We were married two years later. Billy, our first son, arrived in 1965. One night in the year that followed I dreamt I was looking down at a casket. I was unable to identify the person. The face was blurred. I heard sobs and moans in the background. When I awoke, the strong scent of flowers filled the room. A few weeks later, Dad died. He'd been in pain most of his life. His lungs and other parts of his body had always given him a problem. I'm sure he also relied on alcohol to relieve his misery.

Dad was only fifty-five when he died from a stroke. His brother was forty-five when he committed suicide. Both brothers had many problems in life.

Billy and I stayed with Mom for a couple of weeks after the funeral, helping get clothes ready for goodwill and giving her comfort as she grieved. She and Bill became good friends, a friendship that lasted until she died.

## Dad's Poem
### Dedicated to dad

I used to cry for that little girl,
But now I cry for him.
Pain and hurt I'm sure he felt,
Knowing that's what his daddy did to him.

Dad will always be in my heart.
I'll cherish our childhood together.
He didn't have a choice, you know,
Of loving and giving to others.

He will always be my dad.
I choose to love forever.
And as I grow, even loving more,
Dad and I will grow together.

The next year Rick came to us and then Kris. We had three children under five years of age. Our lives were busy yet very happy.

I had become a member of Chuck's church when we married. His family were charter members.

We hadn't been to church for a few months and one Sunday afternoon a church member visited us asking for a pledge of money to the church. Chuck replied, "at the moment we're not able to give a pledge." The man's stern face only focused on

Chuck, never acknowledging me or the children playing on the floor.

"Since you're not pledging, you're costing us money and we're taking you off our books." He abruptly turned and left. Chuck and I were so shocked and embarrassed by the church member's actions.

# Thoughts Control Our Lives

Thoughts are prayers. "For he that thinketh in his heart, so is he" (Proverbs 23:7).

Thoughts begin from childhood. Some are beneficial while others cause hate and resentment. Everyone we know molds our personality with their thoughts.

*Results from Positive Thoughts*

- Loving myself
- Being healthy
- Loving others
- Getting a raise
- Accepting promotion
- Happiness
- Being worthy
- Courage
- Being positive

- Release the past
- Peace of mind

Results from Negative Thoughts

- Fear
- Sadness
- Failure
- Guilt
- Hate
- Revenge
- Resentment
- Sickness
- Rejection
- Frequent accidents
- Being judgmental
- Feeling Unworthy

I only listed a few things that can result from our thoughts. All thoughts or beliefs can be changed by using affirmations of, "I am."

# I Believe

---✦---

There is a power within—call it God, universal mind, or Buddha.

Our first thoughts come from parents, teachers, church groups, and those we know in our childhood days. Many of those thoughts become beliefs.

God doesn't punish. I punish myself, usually from guilt planted within.

God is love. He is with me always and answers all questions.

Thoughts are prayers.

Sickness is caused by hate, resentment, guilt, and other negative thoughts.

Thoughts control destiny, prosperity, health, and well-being.

I am only responsible for myself.

We are all equal.

Being determined has motivated me to make changes in my life.

By making changes in my life, I have found happiness and peace.

I believe in miracles.

God answers all prayers.

Forgiving myself and others and also releasing the past creates love, health, and peace within.

I receive only what I give.

God is love and never criticizes me.

I believe in finding the positive in all situations and accepting myself and others.

I am worthy, and I am healed. (This needs to be repeated many times each day.)

My spiritual growth will continue until I leave this planet (working each day on improving).

Anything is possible.

All events in life happen for a reason.

Christ consciousness can be obtained.

Whatever I give in life will be returned to me.

## *God Accepts All Beliefs*

God accepts us as we accept ourselves. In other words, if a victim blames others for his failures, does not take responsibility for his life, and constantly wants others to give to him, God accepts him and loves him, even though the victim does not have a good image of himself.

I believe if everyone loves themselves and forgives, life on this planet can be a wonderful experience.

I'm not on a mission to change others. I am telling my story of accomplishment and my first steps of living a better life free of heartache.

As I worked with affirmations and meditations, I could feel changes and small miracles happening. Before my change, I had always said positive words, but my thoughts weren't always positive. Now I know the following scriptures are true.

"The kingdom of heaven is within" (Luke 17:21).

"For as he thinketh in his heart so is he" (Proverbs 23:7).

"And my God will supply every need of yours according to his riches" (Philippians 4:19)

# *Part 2*

# Meditation

I learned meditation and affirmation in 1970.

Several girls from the class organized a weekly meeting. We exchanged ideas and books and had a fun girls' night out. I wasn't aware it was the beginning of a new world for me.

Chuck's mom called me one morning asking if I would make an appointment for her to see my doctor. She told me about pain in her back, and she needed a second opinion.

I assured her I would make the appointment and told her everything would be okay. As soon as our conversation ended, I relaxed and my mind was in the meditation state.

I saw her on the stage (in my mind), and Mom's lungs were black. I didn't know why!!

After returning from my meditation state, I called the doctor. The appointment was made, and I talked to the doctor about Mom's situation.

In completing the conversation, I said, "Doctor, please check her lungs."

She was diagnosed with cancer of the lungs. Mom was said to have one year to live. She died in three months. I asked the doctor, "Why? Why did she die? You predicted a year." The family couldn't understand why she left us so soon.

After I confronted the doctor, his answer was, "Fear killed your mother-in-law."

I missed our weekly chats, and I continued caring for the children and studied meditation. I also took writing classes and had a few pieces published.

Thirty years after Dad died, my mom sold her home and spent the summer months with Charles on his farm in Indiana. In the winter she lived with us. We shopped and ate lunches out, or she would bake bread and cook me meals I loved as a child.

After four years Mom was diagnosed with dementia. We moved her to the masonic home near Charles's farm. During the end of her sickness, Mom was sleeping most of the time. At one of our last visits, Mom was coherent.

"Mom, I love you."

"Kathryn, I love you. I told one of the nurses my daughter is beautiful."

Tears came to the surface, and I began to cry as my mom closed her eyes. We will miss Mom, especially the little girl back in that small town in Indiana who needed to hear those words many years ago.

Dedicated to Mom
Thank you, Mom, I understand;
You worked hard to raise your children,
Skimping and saving all you could, never, ever
Complaining.

You did all that was expected of you,
just as Grandma taught you.
You paid the bills, cooked, and baked
and planned the entertainment.

You even opened a business. Most women
wouldn't have the courage.
And today I see you at the sink saying, "Kathryn, set the table."

# My First List of Affirmations

I am determined. I am blessed.

I am healthy. I am accepting myself.

I am worthy. I am slim.

I am prosperity. I am loving myself.

I am giving. I am wealthy.

I am receiving. I am beautiful.

Say each affirmation with enthusiasm, believing you have already received. Say them, scream them, or laugh as you repeat them. Be happy, and know they are true now.

How many times have you said, "I am stupid," "I am miserable," or "I am cheap"? Now is the time to replace the old programing with what you truly desire.

Use "I am" _____.

Never use "not" or "I don't want to."

I am sure you are ready to begin your list of changes.

*Enjoy*

> I am the vine ye (are) the Branch: He that abideth in me
> and I in him, the same bringeth much fruit: for without
> me ye can do nothing. (John 15:5)

> Ask and it shall be given to you. (Matthew 7:11)

*Loving Myself*

Life never worked for me. I had to sort through beliefs and old
ideas. Did I hate? Did I love? I knew I wasn't perfect, and I was
sure I didn't love myself. Always think of others before myself was
my old programing. Time was spent making sure my husband,
children, neighbors, and "Joe Blow" in another city were happy
before I thought of my own well-being.

When I was a child, my mom said, "Be someone." She repeated
that seven to eight times a week. I often wondered what she was
saying. I understand now, I was no one until I began loving
myself.

It starts by affirming.

*I am loving myself.*
*I am loving myself.*
*I am loving myself.*
*I am loving myself.*

It may not feel good at first. If so, repeat:
*I am choosing to love myself.*
*I am choosing to love myself.*

After fifty times, repeat again:
*I am loving myself—singing, screaming, laughing.*

Say it in your prayers.
Say it while in meditation.
Say it every day, all day!

> Imagination is more important than knowledge.
> —Albert Einstein on science

We learn every day how to use our first computer or maybe even how to build a boat. We need directions usually, but the next time, every time, everything is easy. The process takes desire, imagination, and action before the project is started. Whether baking a cake or cleaning a closet, the end results are seen in your mind before the job is started.

When babies learn to walk, they will fall many times, yet determination and imagination keep them trying again and again until their goal is mastered.

Bill was six when I was asked to help him learn to ride his new bicycle. Like all moms, I didn't want him to get hurt, so I taught him how to jump from the bike when he fell. "Mom, I want to ride, not fall." Bill's desire was achieved that afternoon.

Rick was four and a half when we lost him in the forest preserve at Chuck's company-sponsored picnic. We called his name several times, and at last he came running to us crying, "A lion chased me, and a bear tried to get me." We calmed him and soon enjoyed the picnic. As we left, he looked at Chuck's new boss, who was somewhat heavy, and asked, "Are you on a diet?" Weeks after the incident, Rick cried one day, realizing he had not seen the animals. He sobbed, believing he had lied. I'm sure Rick did imagine those animals. Most children would at four and a half years old.

> You are the light of the world, let your light so shine. (Matthew 5:14)

Dedicated to Our Children and Our Grandchildren

A frozen window pane
Brings memories to me
Of my childhood in 1943.
There I stood at the window,
Looking through the glass,
Eager to live,
Eager to love,
Eager to laugh.
As years go by, perhaps in '55,
Daydreams became childish.
Cold facts—knowledge,
Just a frozen window pane.

Now in '77 I've recaptured my dreams.
I've recaptured the scene.

Here I stand at the window,

Looking through the glass,

Eager to give,

Eager to love,

Eager to laugh.

Written by Kathryn Bonney, published by A
DIFFERENT DRUMMER in 1977.

## *Truths*

What I choose to believe is my truth, and what you choose to believe is your truth. There is no right or wrong.

Churches have different truths, and many people are looking for the right truth. There are attitudes of, "If you don't believe my way, you are wrong," and others who respect others' beliefs and their ways of worshiping as well. I was raised by old beliefs. Some were good, like love, giving, praising our creator, and helping neighbors. I wasn't taught to love myself or feel worthy of receiving or how to forgive myself and others. I've spent years meditating, saying affirmations, and now I've gained the feeling of worthiness, loving myself and others, releasing some horrible events in my life, and most importantly, finding the power within.

I believe in the Ten Commandments (Exodus 20).

My love has grown for Chuck and my family.

I looked in the mirror and repeated my affirmations many times until I was convinced. I believe loving myself was my first step for a happier life.

Every day I say, "Kathy, you're great," and I have more love for others.

I make a conscious effort to remember, "Love isn't love until you give it away."

## Seeking Approval

During my childhood, I needed Dad's approval. He never put his hand on my shoulder or kissed or hugged me.

I was hurt to realize dads of my friends treated their daughters with love, held their hands as they crossed the street, and talked with them.

I also had determination in those days, and I worked harder at getting my dad's approval by kissing his cheek, rubbing his back, or trying to have a father/daughter talk. Most of the time I was rejected.

When I entered adulthood, I found I had many of Dad's illnesses and beliefs. I had become that person who had hurt me many times, and I was filled with guilt and resentment.

Resist not evil (Matthew 5:39). Renounce evil, taking your attention from it. When you resist evil, you give it all your attention.

I really experienced hell on earth until I found meditation and affirming. Good changes in my mind were the opportunity I needed for a better life.

I decided to be happy and healthy. The work took a while, but it was worth every minute.

In the beginning of my journey, I stayed clear of medicinal conversations (i.e., "What medicines do you take?"). I also avoided comments like, "Isn't it a horrible day?" Now I am comfortable with negatives. I can find opportunities for positive remarks and have friendly conversation.

*I have learned to:*

- say what's on my mind.
- stand up for myself.
- accept myself and others.
- say how I believe.
- follow my instincts.
- meditate, pray, and say affirmations each day.
- give and receive in my marriage.
- love my parents.
- love myself and others.
- feel God within.

- laugh more.
- believe in myself.
- cry for joy.
- find the positive in every issue.

# Prosperity

*Prosperity can be:*

- winning the lotto.
- having a loving family.
- advancement in career.
- money or gifts.
- a new home.
- receiving a thank you.
- An idea for a business.
- completing a goal.
- acts of kindness.
- starting a new job.
- an opportunity for college.
- winning a trip.

Before you receive prosperity, you must feel worthy of receiving.

Affirm, "I am worthy. I am worthy. I am worthy."

If you feel uncomfortable, try saying, "I choose to be worthy. I choose to be worthy. I choose to be worthy."

After fifty times, repeat, "I am worthy. I am worthy. I am worthy."

## *I Am Worthy*

Say, "I am worthy" at least four hundred times a day while on a treadmill or doing chores. "I am prosperous" will begin the next day. Say those words two to three hundred times each day.

Chuck received a free haircut coupon from a stranger while sitting in the barber's chair. The same day we received two unexpected checks in the mail.

Our world has completely changed, knowing we are worthy to receive.

## *Limitations*

We have all experienced limitations in our lives at one time or another. Sometimes it is called money management to save for a big item, and other times it is a daily routine.

Old beliefs may be:

- I don't deserve it.
- I'll never be rich.

- I'm always unhappy.
- Money is evil.
- I'll die still working.
- I'm always sick.
- I'll never have money.
- I'll never learn.
- I'm poor.
- I'm not worthy of anything.

*Do you limit yourself from having the following:*

- Money
- A better job
- Nice clothing
- Happiness
- Healthy food
- Friends
- Entertainment
- Enjoying life
- Good restaurants
- Relationships

Your body needs the following:

- Facials
- Daily vitamins
- Nail care
- Wonderful clothes
- Hair care

- Pedicures
- Body massage
- Healthy food
- Healthy skin
- Dental visits
- Vitamin D from the sun
- Wellness check-ups

## Worthy of Receiving

There have been many things I wanted in life, yet I never thought I deserved them. Fear of what people thought was foremost in my mind.

When the decision to change my thought process was made, I was determined to whip out these negative and start affirming the good.

I began this affirmation:
I am worthy now.
I am worthy now.
I am worthy now.
I am worthy now to be receiving.
I am worthy now to receive all that is good in life.

Now when I shop, I don't limit myself to the clearance rack, but before leaving the store I always peek at the reduced items. Bargains were a part of my life for years.

## Tears

My tears were never released. Since my childhood days of whipping, Dad threatened to whip harder if I cried. I'm not sure if he was trying to make me strong or if the screams irritated him.

Since I've forgiven my dad during meditation sessions and let go of the hate and the past, my health has improved. I feel joy and peace within and I cry many times a day, especially when I think of Dad. He, too, was whipped as a child and needed to love himself.

I believe my built-up tears have caused glaucoma. I've worked on them and know my eyes have improved.

Tears are good for the soul.

## Habits

Habits can be controlled by the mind, but if drugs are the problem, I suggest asking a doctor's help first. Weight, smoking, and other minor problems can be solved by making a decision to change (determinations) your imaginations (see the habit already corrected) and then act.

I love to eat. Therefore I had a problem. I saw the scale at 150 pounds (in my mind). I saw the dress size I was going to wear (in my mind). I imagined my angel who is always near me removing the taste buds for candy, starches, and colas.

I ate four to five small meals a day, ate no snacks before going to bed, and had cereal (fiber) and fruit for breakfast. I ate popcorn with olive oil for lunch. Oh yes—make a big bowl. I had a small apple with peanut butter for snack in the afternoon. For dinner I had green veggies, a baked sweet potato with a small pat of butter and no brown sugar, and a small piece of meat.

Once a week I cheated, eating anything I wanted at one meal. I saw myself in a size 10 and said affirmations of, "I am," I continued to exercise daily, and the pounds dropped off.

## Criticism

### Self-Criticism

Parents criticized us as children, and we've all had critical bosses.

The more we hear criticism, the more we criticize ourselves.

These seeds are buried in our subconscious, and we can help them escape by praising ourselves and most importantly affirming, "I am loving myself."

A few months ago, I was working in the kitchen and knocked a pan off of the counter. I heard Mom say, "I get so mad at myself." I nearly jumped out of my shoes. I laughed and said to myself, "Mom, you're wonderful, and so am I."

## Compliments

Compliments are giving.

I always compliment a friend on a piece of clothing, jewelry, or tie that I admire. It makes them feel good. After they say, "Thank you," I say, "You're welcome."

In the past I would give compliments but never said, "You're welcome" when a person said, "Thank you." I would say, "No problem" or "That's okay." In other words I was saying, "You're okay; I'm not!" That's exactly how I felt until my beginning of meditation and affirming.

For as he thinketh in his heart, as is he. (Proverbs 23:7)

## Television Can Program Our Minds

All TV programs are filled with negative emotions. Commercials can be the worst, especially when senior citizens are told they are going to fall this year and nobody will be around to help them. They either believe all seniors fall and that's the way it is or they're so frightened they remain in bed for the rest of their lives. There are others who enjoy their lives and have determination to control their minds.

When I hear those negatives from television, I erase them from my subconscious and laugh.

## *Forgiveness*

"Say you are sorry."

It's hard for children to say those words if they don't feel sorry, or maybe they say those words because Mom's angry.

I believe there should be a class available to new parents on how to raise your children without taking away their self-esteem or making them feel unworthy of receiving "good" in life. There may, in fact, be classes out there now, but there weren't when I was a young mom.

I feel sincere forgiveness is important for humankind whether it's for spiritual growth or just getting along with your neighbor.

When I learned meditation, it was a new beginning for my life.

> Forgive them for they know not what they do. (Matthew 23:24)

## *Answers*

Where did it all begin?

Where did it all get started?

Is happiness already here?

Is the journey already charted?

I listened to those who had the answers to life's mysterious ways.

I attempted to follow directions, only to find delays.

All questions were not answered, all questions were only questions

And my life was drifting by, waiting for more suggestions

I answered my questions through meditation—even if they didn't agree—and my life is filling with contentment, knowing I am responsible only for me.

Written by Kathryn Bonney

Published by A Different Drummer 1979

## Meditation

Relax in a comfortable chair with your palms turned up. Count from ten to one with your eyes closed and deeply inhaling and exhaling. Your body will relax as you count and focus:

- Toes and feet
- Shoulders
- Legs
- Neck
- Hips
- Ears
- Back

- Chin
- Arms and fingers
- Eyelids

A second try may be required for complete relaxation. Imagine a shelf on one side of your eye as a thought flies through your mind that interferes. Direct the unwanted to sit on the shelf. You are in control of your thoughts. This could take a few days. It has worked for me.

## Meditation with Color

Use the original meditation script when counting from ten to one, taking deep breaths and exhaling. As you relax each part of your body, you will see a color. The rainbow of colors will help you visualize

- Violet
- Indigo
- Blue
- Green
- Yellow
- Orange
- Red

When you reach your state of meditation, you can create your workshop, a bright healing light, and a stage for the person you are either projecting events for or healing.

Instead of a room, imagine sitting under a huge tree overlooking a stream or lake, blue skies and all of nature's beauty.

Imagination will help you become and receive all you desire.

## *Meditation*

I am blessed. I am blessed.

Reach the state of meditation by saying, "I am blessed" from your feet to your eyelids with deep breaths and exhales.

Thank the body for a great performance. Go to each organ and also bones and tissue and give them your blessing.

For instance, say the following:

> Brain: Bless you, and be alert. (Give one positive thought.) Be healthy.
>
> Eyes: I am seeing. My eyes are healing. My eyes see love. My eyes are blessed.
>
> Skin: My skin is smooth, wrinkle-free. My skin is blessed.
>
> Ears: I am hearing, I am hearing. I am blessed. My ears are hearing.
>
> Bones: I am strong. My bones are strong. I am blessed. My bones are blessed.

As you think of each part of your body, also bless and send love and healing:

I am healed.
I am healed.
I am healed.

Thank God at the end of your blessing session.

My mental cleansing of my mind has been essential for my spiritual growth.

Being forgiven by others and forgiving myself and lovingly releasing the past brings me love and peace. I let my mind drift to childhood, young adult, and child-bearing days, making a list of people I must forgive or forgive myself for issues. Answers came. All I had to do was ask.

There are seeds that appear when you least expect them, like the one I buried after I was molested when I was seven years old. I remembered it when I was in my thirties.

When you are ready, go to your meditation state. See the person you are forgiving or asking for forgiveness on the stage. (He or she can be deceased or still alive.) Look into the person's eyes and repeat two to three times, "I forgive you, or please forgive me." Forgive yourself for the negative emotion you've carried within. Do this two to three times, and then say, "I am releasing the past with love." (Do this two or three times until you feel a lightness.) Seeds sometimes have to be worked on more than once.

> Confess your fault to one another and pray for one another, that you may have health. (James 5:16)

## *Burning Hips*

Around the time we moved to Elgin from Des Plaines where our children were born, I experienced pain in my right hip. It was usually in the evening as pressure was placed on it while sleeping. In a few years the light pain developed into a burning sensation.

I slept on my left side, and the hip pain decreased. After a few years the pain began in the left hip, and like the right hip, the burning also tortured me.

My body needed rest, and I needed answers on how to deal with the problem. I started with getting x-rays of both hips. The results were normal. Before returning in the evening, I prayed for the answer. During the day I had asked why and "How can I rid myself of the pain?" I knew my answers would come, and they did—that day!

Dad, my hate! Yes, it was because of the whippings I'd received many years ago. We'd had many forgiving sessions, and I thought the past was released. Now I knew I still resented my punishment by whippings.

I was at a deep meditation state, and my body relaxed. Dad appeared on my stage at my request. I was emotional, and I wanted to forgive him for the hate I carried.

"Dad, I love you. I love you and I forgive you, and I forgive myself for hating you. I ask for your forgiveness. I love you, Dad. I'm releasing the past. I'm lovingly releasing the past."

Tears of love were flowing, and I felt joy and peace. The burning of the hips had vanished. Built-up tears from many years surface each day as I think of God's miracle of healing.

> Therefore I tell you what you ask for in prayer, believe you have received it and it will be yours. (Mark 11:24)

> Let this mind be in you which was also in Jesus Christ. (Philippians 2:5)

> And my God will supply every need of yours according to his riches. (Philippians 4:19)

# Healings

I was diagnosed with emphysema several years ago. My uncle Ed died of the disease, and thoughts of my dad coughing from his lung disease frightened me. Inhalers were used every day. I was conscious of my disease, and my fear made it worse.

My last breathing test score was fifty-two, the lowest I'd received. The doctor told me to stay clear of secondhand smoke, so the first thought that entered my mind was me pushing an oxygen tank on rollers. The use of inhalers were increased, and my fear was still with me.

I was conscious of the humidity and colds, and I was no longer controlling my positive thoughts. I was frustrated. I had slipped into a routine in life that kept me from saying affirmations and meditating faithfully.

As I opened my eyes the next morning, I made a commitment to myself to live until I was one hundred years old (being healthy).

I also began affirming, "I am stomping out fear and doubt." My affirmations were the following:

- I am confident.
- I am worthy.
- I am healed.
- I am blessed.
- I am healthy.

I said these affirmations while visualizing my lungs.

Soon my body had better balance. My eyesight was better, and my lungs were improving. I was feeling great about myself and others.

We took a trip to Florida to visit Charles and Jean in Gainsville. We drove to the coast before starting home when I felt the humidity in the air. I had to use an inhaler, but we enjoyed the much-needed trip.

I was happy with the improvement of my lungs until two days later. During the night, I woke up having a problem breathing. My inhalers were empty, and I knew Chuck would insist on calling the paramedics. I knew God would help me.

I relaxed my body. Even though my breathing was labored, I found myself in the state of meditation. I kept saying to myself, "I am worthy. I am worthy. I am worthy. I am worthy to breathe now. I am worthy to breathe now. I am healed. I am healed. I am healed." I screamed to myself over and over and over again, "I am healed. I am healed. I am healed." I could feel oxygen opening my lungs. What a blessed feeling; what a feeling of love. I am healed. Through my tears of joy, I thanked God many times.

The healing took three or four minutes. I was exhausted and remember my eyes closing, and I slept like a baby. I was completely rested the next morning.

I shared my excitement with Chuck and then remembered a childhood memory. Mom and I were watching Oral Roberts on TV as he was giving a healing session.

"I believe God can heal," I said. Mom gave me one of her beautiful smiles.

A month later I saw Dr. Garb for my routine appointment. He asked me about my lungs.

"My lungs are healed," I said. "'I've been meditating.'"

He looked puzzled. "Are you using your inhalers?"

"I don't need them, Dr. Garb. I am healed."

He still wasn't satisfied. "I suggest you use them."

"No," I replied. "I am healed."

"Well, I want a breathing test on you."

I scheduled a breathing test for Dr. Garb's benefit.

The test took one hour breathing through a tube. The technician was impressed as he compared each test with the former test results "Hey, you're doing great; you're one hundred percent. An excellent job," he said when the test was completed.

A week later I received a call from Dr. Garb's nurse. "Kathryn, I have your results from your test. Dr. Garb says to tell you everything is normal. What happened? A year and a half ago the test was fifty-two, and now it is above normal."

"I've been meditating."

"It's amazing what the mind can do," she replied.

Some call it the mind. Some know it was God

For as he thinketh in his heart, so is he. (Proverbs 23:7)

# *Part 3*

# Spirits

These are factual stories from family and friends.

Our friend Jennie was traveling by car with her family to dine at a restaurant. A car headed in the other direction came into their lane, and she could see an accident happening. She called upon Gabriel for help, asking that passengers of both cars be safe.

Everyone except Jennie was shocked that the accident was only minor and they were able to continue their travel.

Gabriel gave her a sign of health by leaving a feather at her feet as she walked out of the restaurant. She found another one a few feet away.

Jennie attended a funeral, and an angel was sitting on top of the casket during the service. When the casket was lowered into the ground, the angel remained on the casket.

## The Gift of Feathers

Mary Lou Dabbs

Since I was a very small child, I have always believed in the hereafter. Throughout my life I have had many incidents that have confirmed my beliefs. Some were more profound than others, but they always reassured me that I was on the right path with my faith.

My children's father, Jim, died in my arms May 23, 1994. He had lived with pancreatic cancer for sixteen years, and although I felt blessed to have had him for so long, I was grief-stricken when he passed. I know with great certainty that only through the grace of God did I get through that difficult time. I was going through the motions of life, concentrating on keeping my kids safe and on the straight and narrow. I asked for wisdom and strength to see them through their remaining formative years and help for them to make the right decisions.

One morning early at work a coworker and I were talking, and she said "Oh, Mary, look! You have a feather on your shoulder! It must be Jim!"

I was dumbfounded and incredibly comforted by the strange presence of this little feather. Since that day back in 1994, I have had many circumstances where I have been face-to-face with feathers that come to me as a sign that Jim is watching over me and that there is, indeed, an afterlife.

On my granddaughter's first birthday we were putting a "happy birthday" sign into the ground in our front yard. I looked down, and at the tip of my toe was the most beautiful blue feather.

Another time my grammar school classmates organized a fiftieth birthday trip for all of the girls in our class. It was a three-day, much-needed get-away. I remember floating around the pool on my back saying my thank-you prayers. "Oh God, thank you so much for this opportunity. I really needed this." I opened my eyes, and a feather was floating down from the sky and landed right on my arm.

I was going on a business trip and was really nervous about leaving home. As I got to the bottom of the escalator at the airport, I looked down and there was the most beautiful white feather at my feet.

Jim has been gone for more than twenty years, and I continue to see feathers that make his presence known. My grandkids find them and say, "Nana, look, it's Grandpa Jim." My feathers are a comfort to me, and I feel so blessed when they appear. I never know when they will show up. They just do and mostly when I least expect it.

In 2009, I was on a missionary trip in Kenya. We were welcomed by the monks at the Amani Center, which is a monastery in a small village where our team was assigned the task of building two classrooms onto a school. It was May 23, the anniversary of Jim's death. I had said my morning prayers and crawled out of my mosquito net. I brushed my teeth with some bottled water, all the while thinking back to that May 23, 1994, when my husband, Jim, took his last breath. I remembered talking to our parish priest and telling him how I was holding Jim when he passed.

He said to me, "Mary, Jim went from your arms to our Father's. What a wonderful blessing."

As I opened the door to our tiny, modest room, I was trying to focus on the work ahead for the day. I looked down at the floor mat just outside the threshold of the door, and there was a feather.

The little children in Kenya are bright and full of love and wonder. They all speak English and love to learn about Jesus. In 2011 our team went back to the same village to work. We brought little finger puppets, blankets, bubbles, and books for each orphanage we visited. The children sang for us and welcomed us with open arms. One morning we were sanding wood to build some much-needed desks for classrooms at the Vessel of Hope School. A little boy came up to me. He had a feather in his hand.

He said, "This is for you, mum."

I was so taken aback. I put my sand block down and held out my arms and hugged him. I said, "Thank you so much. This makes me so happy. I have great stories about feathers. They are my favorite. I find them all of the time and save every one, so thank you for making me feel so special today."

The little boy smiled from ear to ear. "What is your name?" I asked.

He looked up at me with his big brown eyes and said, "James."

## Kindness

I was told this story in childhood

My mom's dad, Grandpa Lock, cared for a sick neighbor during the 1861 scarlet fever epidemic. Another neighbor had refused to care for the sick gentleman, fearing he would catch the infectious disease.

Because of Grandpa's loving care, his patient recovered after several months. The next week after the recovery, they attended the funeral of the man who had refused to give to his neighbor. He died from scarlet fever.

## Rick's Adventures

Rick owns houses that he rents out. One of his renters moved and left a child's bicycle in the garage. He had seen children playing down the street, so he took the bike to the house and gave it to their father for them to have.

Only a few days after the "for rent" sign was posted, Rich heard from the family he had given the bike to. They wanted a tour of their soon-to-be home. The bike was able to have its original parking space, and Rick was rewarded for his kindness with a new renter.

Rick and one of his friends, Dave, worked at the same company until Rick left to start his own business. They kept in close contact with each other. After several years Dave married and also started his own business. Rick missed his friend and called him one day. Rick was invited over to meet Dave's wife and also met Laura, who has become the love of Rick's life.

## Spiritual Stories

When Chuck was serving in the Korean War, he often had thoughts of his dad who died when Chuck was only fourteen years old. One evening he felt the presence of his dad, and a feeling of peace prevailed from within.

Soon after that event he was on duty on a moonless night. He had a field telephone wire to guide him and stepped out into nothing. He managed to regain his balance. He lost his rifle off the cliff of twenty to thirty feet. The next day he returned to retrieve the rifle, finding the wooden stock broken in half. He knows a great power prevented him from falling.

## Crying Wolf

In 1970 I had a coworker, Rose Mary, who faked heart attacks at least four times a week. She would place her hands on her chest with a distressed look on her face and in a piercing voice would say "I'm having a heart attack." Everyone came to her aid the first few times, and then we would only chuckle.

Rose Mary either craved attention or just wanted to make people laugh. She worked with us for over a year using her act most every day. One afternoon she started again with, "I'm having a heart attack." Everyone either ignored her or smiled to each other. Rose Mary said, "No, I mean it, I'm having a heart attack." The paramedics didn't arrive soon enough to save Rose Mary's life.

The subconscious mind does not have a sense of humor.

## Spirits

My brother Charles and his wife, Jean, bought a thirty-four-acre farm in Indiana in the '70s. The house was one hundred years old, and I'm sure the walls could tell many stories.

Charles was working in the barn one day when his horse got very nervous. He looked toward the animal and saw a hand petting him.

The horse was then calm. Everyone in our family remembers this scary event.

## Spirits

Steve Moran, Brian's brother, passed away several years ago. Brian and Kris were sorry they hadn't been in touch with him before his death.

Steve was a fun uncle, always playing tricks on his nephews and nieces. The memorial service was April 1 (April Fools' Day). The family was at the gravesite, hearts aching for their loved one, and a bird flew over and planted one on Matthew's head.

After Steven's memorial service, Kris dreamed she flew to her mother-in-law's kitchen, where Steve was standing and smiling. Kris said, "We love you." Steven replied, "I am fine." Kris and Brian are thankful their loved one is happy.

## Spirits

Dad's spirit returned to comfort Mom as she was grieving for her loss. She witnessed a glorious light at the end of her bed and heard Dad's voice saying he was fine and she needed to continue her life.

## Spirits

Many months after my mom died, each time I would wake up from a sleep I would see her standing in the middle of the room. My friend suggested I release the spirit into the heavens. I can now feel her happiness.

## Prayers

Our grandson, Jack, plays on the football team in high school. His team is rated number one in the area. Jack loves the game yet needed a boost in his confidence.

Our daughter, Kris, began praying as the team started the game. The prayer was short: "Thank you, God, for giving Jack the confidence to make a touchdown."

She prayed the sentence several times, and just minutes later Jack, indeed, ran that ball down the field for a touchdown. Mom and son smiled through their tears of joy!

## Spirits—Uncle Bill

Chuck's brother, Bill, lived with us when he couldn't care for himself any longer. He had lived by himself for thirty years and didn't like change. He never had a social life, and his habits developed into a "not caring" attitude.

Bill was soon aware of the shower, washing machine, and dryer. Uncle Bill gained weight. He helped Chuck with the yard work and took breaks, sitting on the patio and looking at the pond adjacent to our backyard.

One afternoon when Bill and I were talking, he said it was time to die. "Bill, God gives you what you ask. Are you sure that's what you want?"

"Oh yes, that's what I want," he replied.

I had a feeling Bill's request was going to manifest. Our family had a birthday party for Uncle Bill and our son Bill at a restaurant in the fall. Uncle Bill died the following April at eighty-six years old.

Our clock stopped around the time of his death. Chuck started to replace the batteries when he realized the clock was running. It also had the right time … Strange!

Chuck brought me yellow roses (he always bought me red roses). The buds never opened, and the leaves never fell. They looked the same in two weeks as they did the day I put them in the vase. Uncle Bill?

A piece of ivy was in a glass of water sprouting roots, and I would check it every day to see if it was ready to plant. One morning I found the plant laying on the other side of the sink. I replaced it in the glass and again it was out of the glass the next day.

Uncle Bill was having a great time!

Bill had his apartment downstairs in our home with a bath, a large closet, and a bed in front of the fireplace in our family room. I was staring at the fireplace thinking of Bill when a bright light moved over all of the carpet, under tables, and over a big rocking chair.

Bill is still with us!

I was eating a piece of cheese, and our dog, Henry, begged for his share. I tossed a piece of the cheese to him, and it vanished in midair I tossed another piece, and it also vanished. Henry was searching on the floor for his cheese, and so was I.

Uncle Bill loves a good joke.

Chuck was reading in his chair when he felt a hand on his shoulders. He told me about it the next morning.

We felt Uncle Bill soon would be leaving.

After Uncle Bill's death, it appears he joined us at a family dinner at Kris and Brian's home. Kris cooked a great meal for fifteen people. The adults sat at the dining room table, and the young group ate in the kitchen. Bill had his own calling card when he was alive. He wore a catheter, and sometimes it leaked. Only two of the family members smelled the odor at that family dinner, one from each table. These two were the ones who weren't sure if Uncle Bill had returned.

Bill's ashes were placed in the pond near us. He is close to the flowers he watered every summer. We see the pond from our home, and we all have a feeling of love and peace.

## Plants Need Positive Thoughts

We gave Ann Boss, our friend, an orchid from Uncle Bill's memorial service. She talks to her new plant every morning, saying he is wonderful and healthy. The beautiful orchid is called Uncle Bill and thrives from her loving attention.

A Boston fern in her yard was turning yellow and close to dying. She placed the plant on her patio, where she talks and admires the growing fern. Ann's kind words have given her a huge, healthy plant.

Chuck and I have large tomatoes, cucumbers, and peppers. Chuck loves working in the yard and garden.

My African violets are healthy and blooming. This is one of my hobbies I've enjoyed for fifty years.

## Energy Level

I believe when my energy level is low, it's usually because my body needs rest or sometimes I have entertained negative thoughts. I ask myself, "Have I been scolding myself?" Perhaps I've neglected a routine of spiritual growth (meditation and saying affirmations).

I was washing windows one day, and I stumbled and fell to my knees. I became critical of myself. I was working on, "I am balance. I am strong. I am strength."

Of course the fall didn't hurt me and I turned my determinations on high; then the energy level increased, and now I am stronger. I have more strength, and my balance is better. I feel twelve years younger.

## *Receiving Answers*

*I receive answers from the following sources:*

> Prayers: Thank you for showing_____.

> Affirmation: I am receiving.

> Sleep on it: Ask for answers just before sleeping.

> Dream: Ask for answers, and many times the answer comes in a dream. If interested, study dream books.

A favorite is asking myself, "Where are my keys?" I see them in my mind or will be led to them.

Another is, "Where is the (item)?" and the item comes in my mind. I see where I misplaced it or I am led to it.

I always find a close parking place when I am shopping or eating out. I program my mind, "I am finding a parking space closest to the entrance." (I visualize the spot.) This is really great if it's raining!

You may find ways that work better. Read other viewpoints, and practice all. Notice your feelings. Let them show you. Do you trust yourself? In other words, use your instincts, and listen for the feeling of "I know that I know."

## Enjoy the Trip

Chuck came from an organized family. In fact, before we were married, he said he liked a house that was "lived in." He was marrying the right gal because I thought I'd rather paint a room than clean a medicine cabinet.

I did all the painting. He paid bills and made lists of things he should do. After several years of accomplishing all of these "do this and do that" lists, he worried about being perfect instead of enjoying his family.

He placed a huge sign that read, "Enjoy the Trip" on the ceiling above our bed. Before he slept at night and when he awakened he read the sign, and these words were passed on to his subconscious mind.

Signs were placed on bathroom mirrors and refrigerators. When we needed a new car, a picture of a car, color, and model was taped on a door of the cabinet in the kitchen. Our car appeared in a few weeks, and Chuck's sign "Enjoy the Trip" helped him enjoy his family.

## Routine for a Happy Life

Each morning as I awake, my thoughts are on a beautiful day ahead of me. My prayers take me to my state of meditation, thanking God for my answered prayers and thanking him for things yet manifested.

## Exercise

The treadmill is the next routine for me and also walking my dog for a mile or more. Other exercise could be golf, tennis, swimming, or dancing. Kris likes golf, paddle tennis, and running. Bill and Rick like fishing, golf, and working out at the health club.

## Vitamins

Most bodies need a good vitamin supplement. Health food stores can give you information. I take an herbal supplement.

## Eating

Eating habits in our home consist of many fruits and vegetables. Diet pop is a no. Instead we choose caffeine-free coffee or tea. We eat whole grain cereals and a small amount of meat. Dairy food is popular. For the last ten years, baked sweet potatoes have replaced the regular baked potato with lots of sour cream. Popcorn with a few drops of olive oil is also a great lunch and an apple with peanut butter spread on the slices for an afternoon snack.

If I eat bread, it is only one piece. I have cut out potato chips completely.

I meditate three times daily. I say affirmations almost all day when driving, on treadmill, or walking. Most days I discover an old thought that needs to be forgiven and released.

# Unity

Unity Church of Fox Valley is friendly. We received greetings of love and were happy to hear the five musicians play their instruments as their beautiful voices sang in praise.

Rev. Jan Little gives meditations and the message each Sunday. The Lord's Prayer is sung, the daily word is read, and the affirmation of "Wherever we are, God is and all is well." is said.

There are many Christian churches and also Buddhists and metaphysics, such as Unity and Science Of The Mind. Visit a few until you find the one that helps your spiritual growth. I believe spiritual growing takes seven days a week until I leave this planet.

I never understood the Bible. The only word I heard was *fear*. Now I believe *love* is the only word I hear. I now have the tools I need to experience spiritual growth.

# Prayers

The kingdom of heaven is within you. (Mark 7:21)

## Lord's Prayer

Our father which art in heaven, hallowed be thy name. Thy kingdom come, thy will be done on earth as it is in heaven. Give us this day our daily bread and forgive us our debts as we forgive our debtors and lead us not into temptation but deliver us from evil: for thine art the kingdom and the power and the glory forever. Amen.

## Prayer

Dear God, I asked for a better life and you led me to the answers. Thank you, thank you. I give you praise for healings and techniques I use for forgiveness and release from negative thoughts and acts. Thank you for your guidance and love and my tears of joy. Amen.

Dear God, thank you for this beautiful day and your love, miracles, and forgiveness. Thank you for the opportunity to release old beliefs that kept me from loving myself and others. These old beliefs imposed sickness in my body. I know my prayers are answered by my Father, and I give you the praise. Thank you for your guidance toward knowledge that speeds my spiritual journey. Amen.

These are the prayers I say three or four times a day. The love, emotion, and many thanks will increase awareness of needed changes by affirming and forgiving yourself and others by meditation.

I believe all prayers are answered. It could take weeks, months, or years. If you doubt, ask yourself these questions:

- Do I feel anything is possible?
- Do I feel worthy of receiving?
- Need I forgive others or myself?
- Do I need to release a past issue?
- Are my prayers positive?
- Do I say thank you to God within?
- Do I pray for others?
- Is love in my heart when I pray?

God has answered all of my prayers. A few times years went by before I witnessed a prayer's manifestation for me. They happened at the right time for more spiritual growth.

# To My Readers

Our family has had several crises, yet God has never said no to my prayers and dreams.

In the '70s my dream was to write a book. I thought of the dream many times, but raising my children and with my questions, "What would I write?" "What's important?" and "Do I know?" I put it on hold.

This dream came true, and while telling my story I conquered that hidden seed I was unaware of.

My prayer is that you, too, have many awakenings and your desires will be to continue your journey.

This book began with a thought in the '70s.

Dream, dream, always dream, and the hows and whys will come. As you travel in time your dreams will manifest.

# Bible Verses

---

God created man in his own image. (Genesis 1:27)

I am the vine ye (are) the branches: He that abideth in one and I in him the same bringeth much fruit: for without me ye can do nothing. (John 15:5)

Jesus saith unto him I am the way, the truth and the life; no man cometh unto the Father, but by me. (John 14:6)

Ask and it shall be given to you; seek and you shall find; knock … (Matthew 7:7, 11)

The thoughts of the righteous are right. (Proverbs 12:5)

For as he thinketh in his heart, so is he. (Proverbs 23:7)

The kingdom of heaven is within you. (Luke 17:21)

But they who wait for the Lord shall renew their strength; They shall mount up with wings as eagles; they shall run and not be weary; and they shall walk, and not faint. (Isaiah 40:31)

You are the light of the world ... Let your light so shine. (Matthew 5:14, 16)

Confess (your) fault to one another and pray for one another, that ye may have health. (James 5:16)

If thou canst believe, all things are possible to him that believeth. (Mark 9:23)

Be not overcome with evil, but overcome evil with good. (Romans 12:21)

Let this mind be in you which was also in Jesus Christ. (Philippians 2:5)

And the peace of God which passes all understanding shall keep your hearts and minds through Jesus Christ. (Philippians 4:7)

If you do not forgive others their trespasses, neither will your Father forgive your sins. (Matthew 6:15)

Forgive them for they know not what they do. (Luke 23:24)

You shall love your neighbor as yourself. (Matthew 23:39)

Therefore I tell you whatever you ask for in prayer, believe you have received it and it will be yours. (Mark 11:24)

Resist not evil, but I tell ye not to resist an evil person but whoever slaps you on your right cheek, turn the other to him also. (Matthew 5:39)

Seek ye the kingdom of God, and his rightness, and all these things will be provided for you as well. (Matthew 6:33)

But one thing I do, forgetting the things which are behind and stretching forward in the things which are before. I press on towards the goal. (Philippians 3:13)

All things were made by him; without him was not anything made that was made. (John 1:3)

Judge not according to the appearance but judge rightness judgement. (John 7:24)

Thou shall love the Lord thy God with all thy heart, soul, mind and strength and they neighbor as thyself. (Mark 12:30–31)

Be ye doers of the word and not hearers only, deceiving themselves. For if any be a hearer of the word and not a doer, he is like a man beholding his natural face in a glass, and on going away, forgets what a manner of man he was, but who so looketh into the perfect lay of liberty and continues therein, he being not a forgetful hearer but a doer of the word, this man shall be blessed in his deed. (James 1:22–25)

## Books to Read and Study

*You Can Heal Your Life*
By Louise L. Hay of the Hay House
Louise Hay has other books available

*In the Flow of Life*
By Eric Butterworth of Unity

*Unity, a Quest for Truth*
By Eric Butterworth
Eric Butterworth has other books available

*The Tapping Solutions for Pain Relief*
By Nick Ortner of Hay House

*Power of Awareness*
Also includes awakened imaginations
By Neville Tarcher, Cornerstone Editions

You will find other metaphysics books to study!


*Enjoy the trip!*

Printed in the United States
By Bookmasters